MW01015671

This book is a republishing of the 1965 English version of *Norsk Strikkemønstre* by Annichen Sibbern Bøhn, originally published in Norwegian, in 1929 by Grøndahl & Son Publishers, Oslo, Norway. Includes all charts from the 1965 edition, plus figs 64-68, 72-77 from the 1945 Norwegian edition, which were omitted in English to make room for the sweater patterns.

Thanks to Annichen's children, Annichen Bohn Kassel, Sidsel Bohn Kringstad, and Ole Anders Bohn, for permission to republish.

Photos, chart editing and revising by Terri Shea.

This edition published by

Spinningwheel LLC
PO Box 30863
Seattle, WA 98113

http://www.norwegianknittingdesigns.com/

ISBN 978-0-9793126-1-8

NORWEGIAN
KNITTING DESIGNS

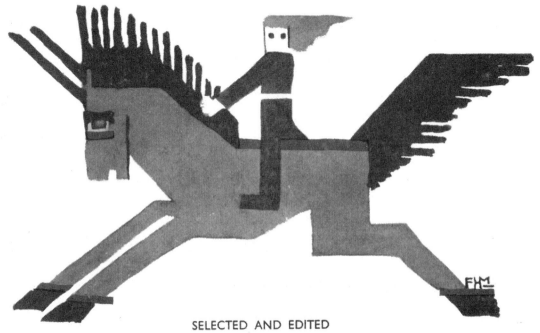

SELECTED AND EDITED

WITH AN INTRODUCTION AND DESCRIPTIONS

BY

ANNICHEN SIBBERN BØHN

Spinningwheel LLC
Seattle, Washington

FOREWORD

This book is important.

Historically it is important. Published in 1929, at a time when modernity was rapidly swallowing traditional culture, *Norwegian Knitting Designs* almost single-handedly preserved the old designs and put them in the hands of craftspeople throughout Norway.

Author Annichen Sibbern Bøhn was a young woman, recently out of college, when she travelled across Norway to collect and preserve her nation's knitting history. She was born into a family of high rank and privilege; her father was friends with the man who would become King Olav V. Her mother's family includes the architect who designed the Rådhus, the Oslo City Hall where the Nobel Peace Prize is still awarded, and one of the "Heroes of the Telemark" whose actions in WWII destroyed a Nazi heavy water plant and prevented Hitler from obtaining nuclear weapons. Annichen and her husband Ole Bøhn were themselves active members of the Norwegian Resistance. In addition to spreading resistance information, they hid Jews in their own home to protect them from internment.

The designs in the book are important. Deeply rooted in ancient symbols, Norwegian folk motifs speak to our oldest mental and spiritual beings. We were tool makers and tool users a million years before we could speak, and archaeology has uncovered countless prehistoric items covered with decorative figures. These function in the subconscious like archetypes, working with and providing focus for, deep seated needs and experiences. We communicate with design and color unconsciously, even more than we communicate with words.

This book is important now. Modern culture is being overwhelmed by virtualization. We live in a bath of electronic messages, and we spend increasing amounts of time using our words and our minds, but are neglecting the physical and spiritual realms. We still need to make and use tools, and we need the things we make with those tools. Any mother will tell you of the overwhelming urge to wrap a new baby in beautiful, hand made clothes and blankets. Preferably ones she has made herself, or were made by her closest friends and family. Things matter.

When craftspeople base our work in ancient symbols, we take the cosmic leap from timelessness to transcendence. A rose on a mitten is not just a pretty decoration. It speaks to our deep selves, in a language we have largely relegated to fairy tales. Roses speak of love, romance, seduction, and in Christian iconography, they also can represent Christ or the Virgin Mary. Zigzagging lines represent water, that great realm of the subconscious, the place from which we emerge, and the great unknown to which we will all return. Work a row of dancers holding hands onto a hat for a new baby, and you surround that child with community.

I have several goals in republishing *Norwegian Knitting Designs*. First, to put this too-long out-of-print work back into circulation. The designs are beautiful in their own right, and I know that today's artists, designers, and craftspeople will enjoy using them. Second, to boldly assert that this original work still matters. Annichen wove her private and public lives together, like two colors in a stranded design. Neither existed without the other. After the war, when her children needed her attention, she largely left public teaching and publishing to focus on her family, and she included teaching her daughters to knit in that focus. The book stands as a testament to her work and sacrifice, and that must never be forgotten. Third, to remind modern culture that working with the hands is important. More than important, vital to our well being. We are tool makers and users, and we cannot be healthy unless we make things. And finally, my own need to continue working with the designs that prompted publication of my first book, *Selbuvotter: Biography of a Knitting Tradition*. Ancient symbols are powerful. First they work on you, and then they work in you, and then they work through you. My transformation began with a box of mittens in a small heritage museum. It continues as I use these designs in my own work, and will complete only when you, the audience for whom this book is prepared, use them in yours.

Special thanks go to Annichen Sibbern Bøhn's three children, all of whom are still living. My direct contact Annichen Kassel has lived in the United States since the 1950's. Sidsel Kringstad lives in Norway, and Ole Bøhn lives in Sweden. I am so grateful that you have permitted me to reprint your mother's work. Your kindness and generosity are her greatest legacy.

INTRODUCTION

The country women of Norway faithfully keep alive knitting designs made traditional over the past several hundred years.

Knitting as a handicraft became an important part of life on the farms. During the long, dark Norwegian winters busy hands knit warm and beautiful garments for the family. Knitting is also the pleasant occupation of the woman on the remote mountain seters where the herds are taken to graze during the lonely summer days when the night barely falls.

The national disposition, imaginative designs and a sense of color are apparent in this native handwork and not least throughout the ages knitting has develop into a characteristic Norwegian handicraft.

By making this form of art accessible to the modern knitter we feel we are both preserving and developing it.

Design knitting can be used in many different ways... especially for garments, but handbags, cushions, rugs etc. can be made by combining certain border patterns and designs. However, design knitting is mainly used for caps, mittens, gloves, sweaters, socks and scarves.

The following patterns are drawn on graph paper, each square representing one stitch. Most of these designs are originally knitted in black and white, however various colors can be used. Den Norske Husflidsforening, Oslo (The Norwegian Home Craft Company, Oslo) will send, on request, a selection of color samples. If one is uncertain regarding color combinations it is always safe to stick to black and white.

In order to determine the number of stitches to be cast on for the designs, divide the number of stitches required for the entire work by the number of stitches required in the design. For example one design stitch-count is 8. The number of stitches cast on must be a multiple of 8, such as 56-64-72-80 etc. This rule follows for all designs.

A few words about the method of knitting.

Most people know that the "European" method differs from the "ordinary" method.

Especially in design knitting it is preferable to use the "European" manner if possible. With a little perseverance one will find this method saves time and ensures a more evenly knit garment. The knitter has better control over the tension of the loops of wool drawn between patterns on the reverse side of the work.

The operation is exactly the same in both methods, only the execution differs.

This is how to knit "European": Place the various colors of wool in use over the index finger of the left hand. Hold neither taut or slack. When knitting place the tip of the right needle through the stitch on the left neeedle, but instead of using the right hand to loop the wool over the needles, the needle itself "picks out" the color it needs from the strands drawn over the left index finger. Draw the stitch as usual and slip off tip of left needle.

When one becomes accustomed to this manner of knitting, especially in design knitting, it is surprising how rapidly the work grows under ones fingers.

In knitting waist bands etc. the "ordinary" method can just as well be used.

In order to give a little additional help to those trying design knitting for the first time models and directions are given here.

In design knitting it is essential to remember never to tighten the wool that is carried between patterns on the reverse side of the garment. The beauty and elasticity of the work are both reduced by drawing too tightly.

Design-knit garments involve too much work to be ruined in the first washing, therefore all colors chosen should be colorfast wool, and all of the same thickness.

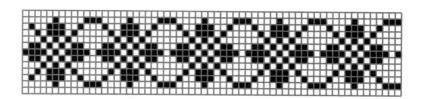

Be careful of color combinations. When in doubt remember that black and white are always attractive, with perhaps a touch of bright red, blue or greeen.

Knitting a garment of the proper size is of course important. The safest way is to use measurements. We all knit differently, the tension can vary considerably, so there is little help in having patterns to follow. To find your own tension knit a small patch with the wool and needles to be used for the garment, press and measure how many stitches equal 1 inch in width and length. By measuring find then the desired size of the garment and calculate how many stitches to cast on, and also how many rows to be knitted.

All designs which are shown in the book can of course be altered to suit other garments than those show in the drawings.

Sportswear should be loose and comfortable. The "Luskofte" show here is 21 inches wide. Using ordinary wool for sportswear and needles number 12, and 6 stitches to the inch we can calculate how many stitches to cast on in this way: 21 inches X 6 = 126 stitches, for the whole sweater that would mean 252 stitches.

But first of all let us take a sample of design knitting and use.

Take two balls of wool in contrasting colors, but of the same thickness. Cast on required number of stitches. This design has a stitch-count of 12... ie, from A-B. From B the pattern is repeated throughout the round.

We must remember that the number of stitches cast on must be a multiple of 12 or else there will be an incomplete design at the join.

The outline of the design proper is made by the black squares. If you wish to knit the design shown below on one round needle, rather than across and back, the method used is as follows:

1st Row: Knit three black stitches, 4 white, 1 black, 4 white, 3 black, 4 white, 1 black, et cetera.

2nd Row: 3 white, 1 black, 2 white, 3 black, 2 white, 1 black, 3 white, 1 black, 2 white, et cetera.

3rd row: 4 white, 1 black, 1 white, 3 black, 1 white, 1 black, 5 white, 1 black, 1 white, et cetera.

4th Row: 5 white, 1 black, 1 white, 1 black, 1 white, 1 black, 7 white, 1 black, 1 white, et cetera.

5th Row: 3 white, 2 black, 1 white, 1 black, 1 white, 1 black, 1 white, 2 black, 3 white, 2 black, 1 white, 1 black, et cetera.

6th Row: 1 black, 1 white, 4 black, 1 white, 1 black, 1 white, 4 black, 1 white, 4 black, 1 white, et cetera.

Then continue knitting acccording to the design drawn below on graph paper.

If for example, you wish the same design in a scarf and knit across and back with two needles, then progress in this manner:

1st Row: Knit 3 black, 4 white, 1 black, 4 white, 3 black, 4 white, 1 black, 4 white, 3 black, 4 white, 1 black, 4 white, 3 black.

2nd Row: Purl 3 white, 1 black, 2 white, 3 black, 2 white, 1 black, 3 white, 1 black, 2 white, 3 black, 2 white, 1 black, 3 white, 1 black, 2 white, 3 black, 2 white, 1 black, 3 white.

3rd Row: Knit 4 white, 1 black, 1 white, 3 black, 1 white, 1 black, 5 white, 1 black, 1 white, 3 black, 1 white, 1 black, 5 white, 1 black, 1 white, 3 black, 1 white, 1 black, 4 white.

4th Row: Purl again, and count the stitches in the design drawing in the same manner. Knit and purl in alternating rows.

Back of
Mitten ⟶

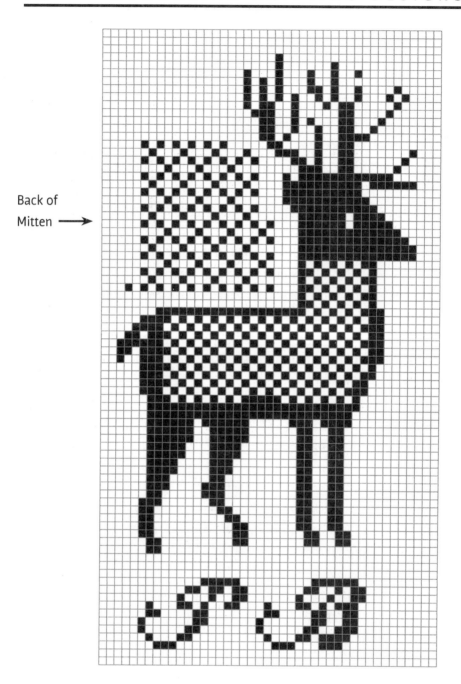

Fig. 1. Design pattern for the accompanying fig. 2.

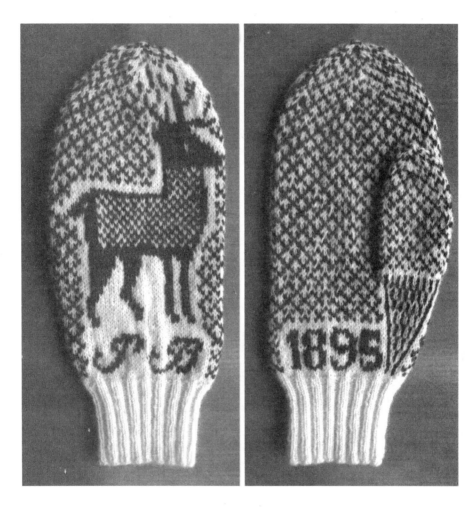

Fig. 2.
MAN'S MITTEN FROM SELBU
See fig. 1 for design pattern.

Fig. 3. Design pattern for the accompanying fig. 4.

Fig. 4. Design for handbag. Sample worked in lavender
background with brown design.

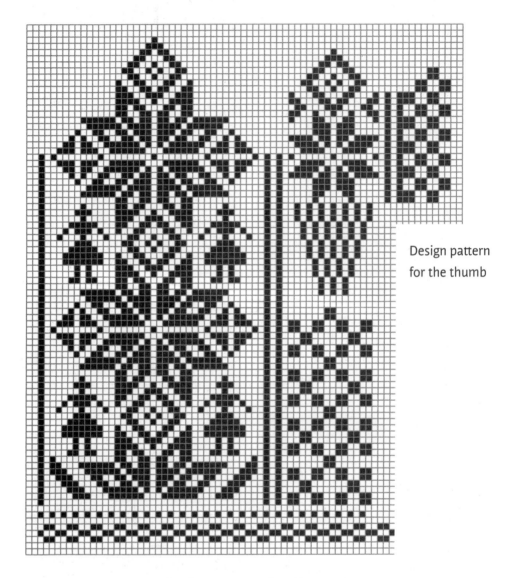

Design pattern
for the thumb

Fig. 5. Design pattern for the accompanying figs. 6 and 7.
Count stitches cast on for mitten 75.

Fig. 6. Back   Fig. 7. Palm

MITTEN FROM SELBU
See fig. 5 for the design pattern.

Fig. 8. Design pattern for accompanying figs. 9 and 10.

Fig. 9. Back   Fig. 10. Palm

MITTEN FROM SELBU
See fig. 8 for the design pattern.

Fig. 11. Design pattern for the accompanying fig. 12.

Fig. 12 MITTEN FROM SELBU
See fig. 11 for the design pattern.

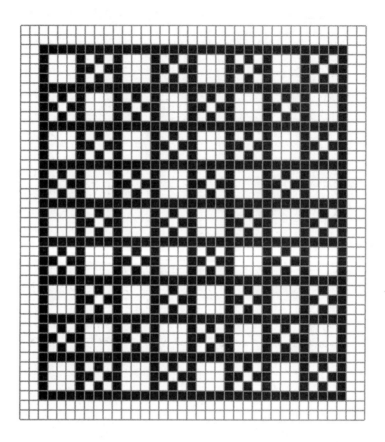

Fig. 13. Design pattern for the accompanying fig. 14.
Each design-segment has 8 stitches.

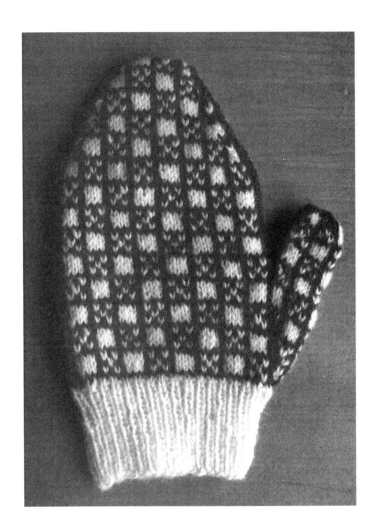

Fig. 14.
CHILD'S MITTEN FROM HALLINGDAL
See fig. 13 for the design pattern.

Fig. 15. Design pattern for the accompanying fig. 16.
Multiple of 12 in Stjerne (Star) border.
102 stitches in calf of medium man's stocking.

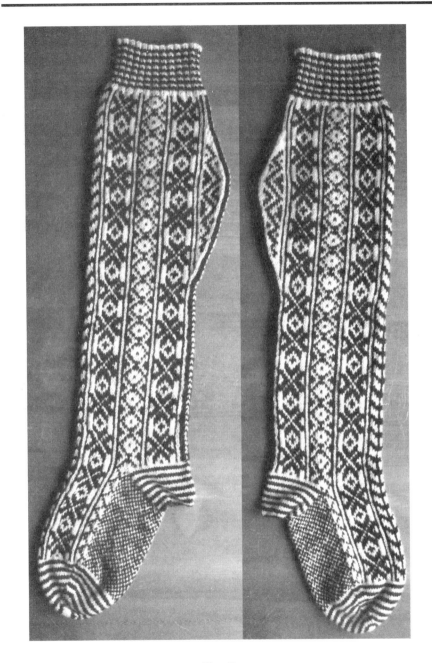

Fig. 16.
STOCKING FROM HALLINGDAL
See fig. 15 for the design pattern.

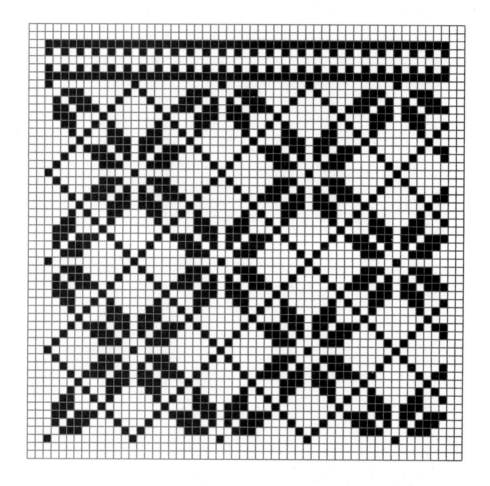

Fig. 17. Design pattern for the accompanying fig. 18.
Each design segment has 22 stitches.

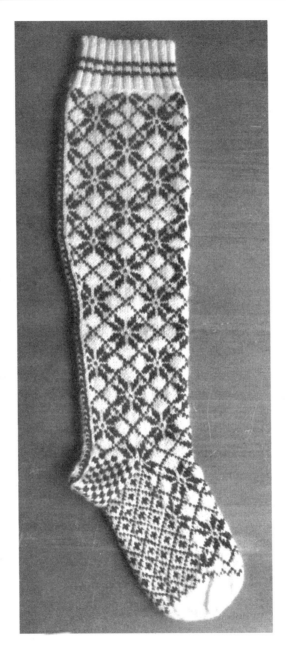

Fig. 16.
STOCKING FROM SELBU
See fig. 17 for the design pattern.

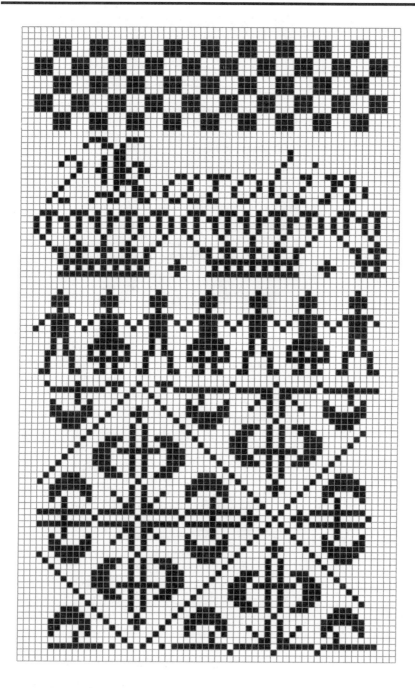

Fig. 19. Design pattern for the accompanying fig. 20.

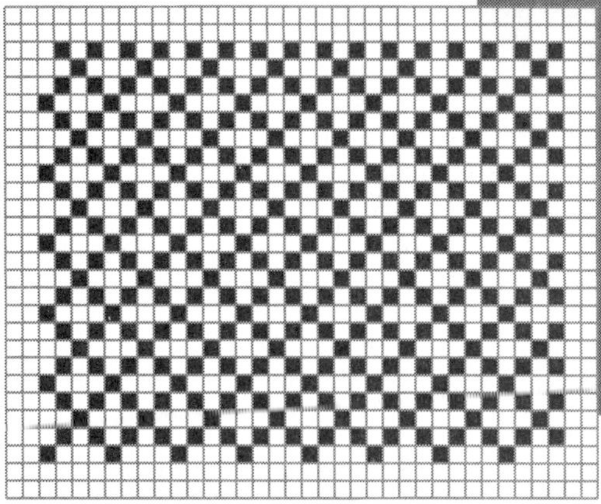

Fig. 20. STOCKING FROM SELBU

See figs 19 and 21 for the design patterns.

Fig. 21. Sole of the foot

Fig. 22. Design pattern for the accompanying fig. 23.
The design's stitch-count is 29.

Fig. 23. STOCKING FROM BØ IN TELEMARK
in blue and white.
See fig. 22 for the design pattern.

Fig. 24. Design pattern for the accompanying fig. 25.
The design's stitch-count is 25.

Fig. 25. STOCKING
See fig. 24 for the design pattern.

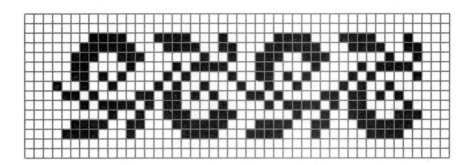

Fig. 26.

Fig. 27. Design pattern for the accompanying fig. 28.

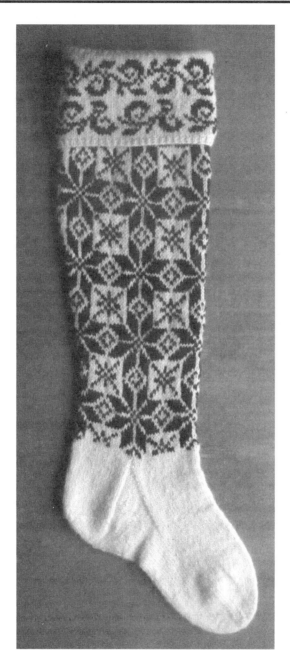

Fig. 28. STOCKING FROM SELBU
See figs. 26 and 27 for the design pattern.

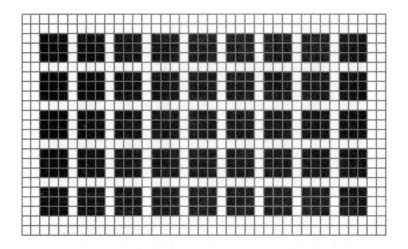

Fig. 29. Design pattern for the acompanying fig. 30.
Each design segment has 4 stitches.

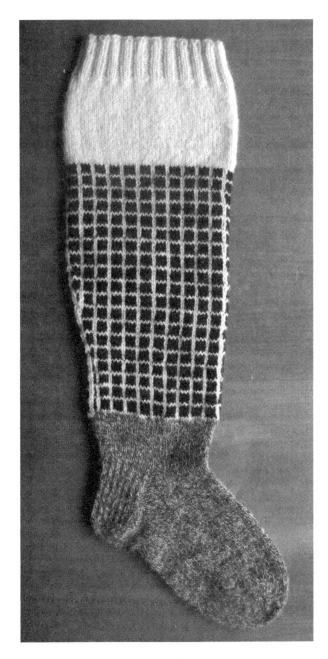

Fig. 30.
STOCKING
See fig. 29 for the design pattern.

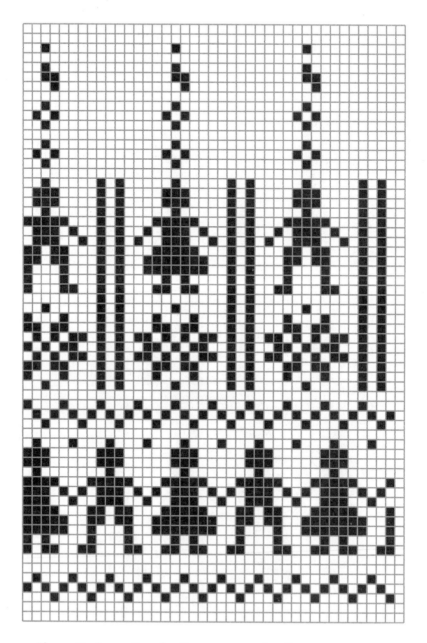

Fig. 31. Design pattern for the accompanying fig. 32.

Fig. 32.
CAP FROM SELBU
See fig. 31 for the design pattern.

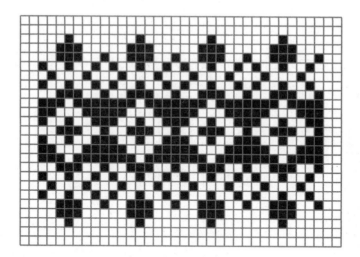

Fig. 33.

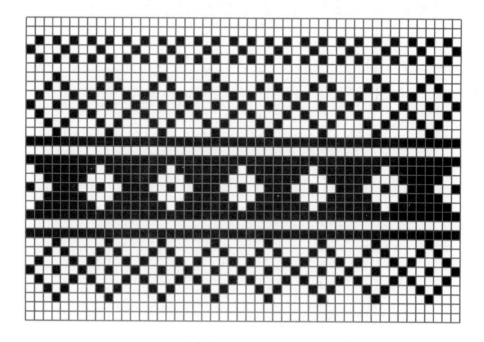

Fig. 34. Design pattern for the accompanying fig. 35.

Fig. 35. GAMMEL TOPPLUE
(Old Stocking Cap)
See figs. 33 and 34 for the design pattern.

Fig. 36. Design pattern for the accompanying fig. 37.

Fig. 37. "LUSKOFTE" FROM SETESDALEN
("Lice Jacket" - the national Ski Sweater.)
See figs. 36, 38, and 39 for the design patterns.

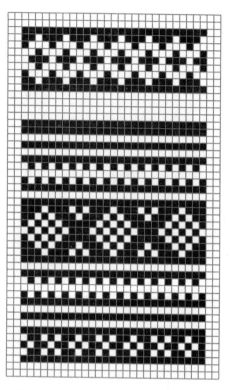

Fig. 38. Design pattern for fig. 37.

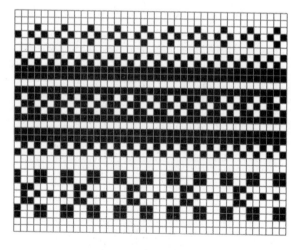

Fig. 39. Design pattern for fig. 37.

Fig. 40.

DESIGN FROM HALLINGDAL

Each design has 18 stitches.

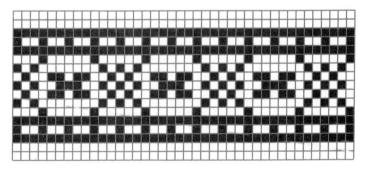

Fig. 41.

BORDER DESIGN

Each design has 12 stitches.

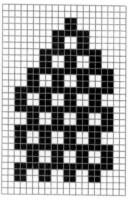

Fig. 42.
MITTEN
FROM JÆREN

Fig. 43.
STAR
FROM SELBU

Design's stitch-count is 31.

Fig. 44.
DESIGN
FROM SELBU

Design's stitch-count is 29.

Fig. 45.
MITTEN FROM SELBU

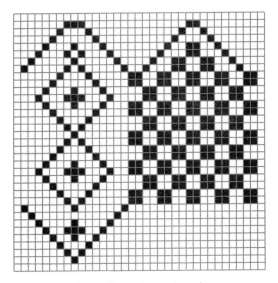

Fig. 46. The Selbu mitten thumb pattern.

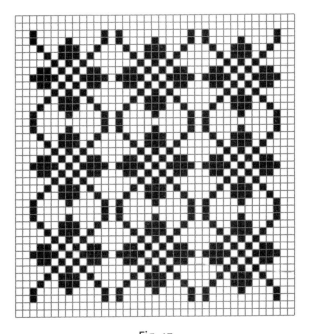

Fig. 47.
SCARF DESIGN
Knit to the desired length and attach fringe to the ends.

Fig. 48. Ornament used with the border below. It may be placed by a low-cut neck, or down by the border design.

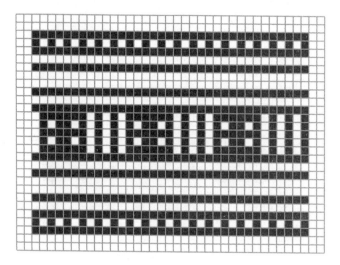

Fig. 49. BORDER DESIGN FOR A CHILD'S SWEATER
Each segment has 11 stitches.

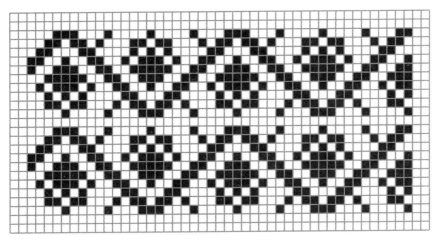

Fig. 50. BORDER

Each design segment has 20 stitches.

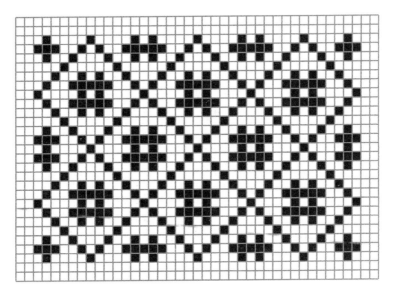

Fig. 51. BACKGROUND DESIGN

Each design segment has 12 stitches.

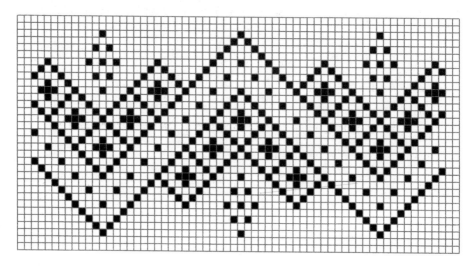

Fig. 52.

BORDER

The design's stitch-count is 40.

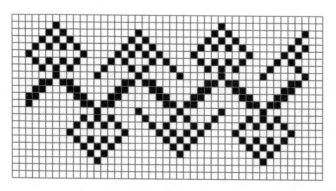

Fig. 53.

BORDER

The design's stitch-count is 24.

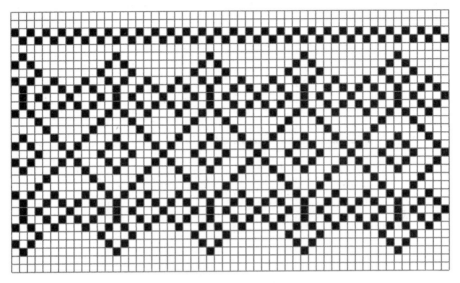

Fig. 54.
BORDER
The design's stitch-count is 12.

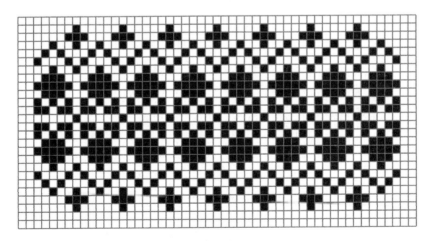

Fig. 54.
BORDER

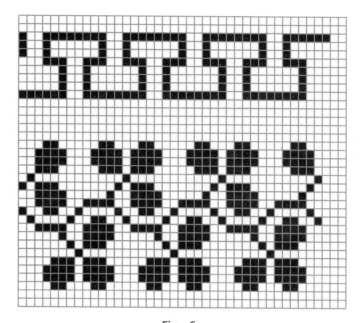

Fig. 56.

DESIGN FROM NORDENFJELSKE

Red background, white design. Design's stitch count is 12.

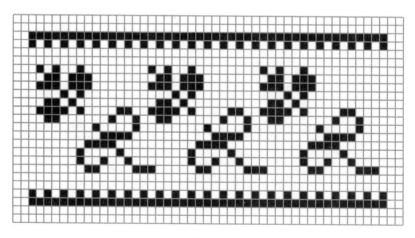

Fig. 57.

SELBU BORDER

Design's stitch-count is 15.

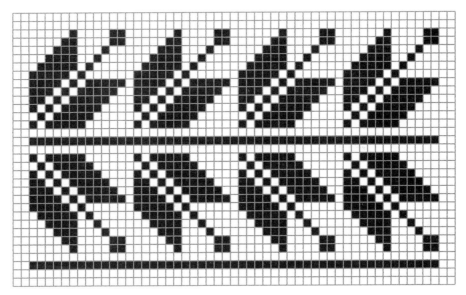

Fig. 58.

HALLING BORDER

Each design segment has 11 stitches.

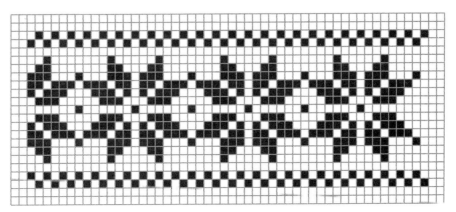

Fig. 59.

SELBU STAR BORDER

Each design segment has 14 stitches.

Fig. 60.

ORNAMENT

The design's stitch-count is 54.

Fig. 61.
BACK OF THE HAND AND BACKGROUND PATTERN
FOR THE HALLING MITTEN.

Fig. 62.
BORDER
Each design has 24 stitches.

Fig. 63.
BORDER
Each design has 27 stitches.

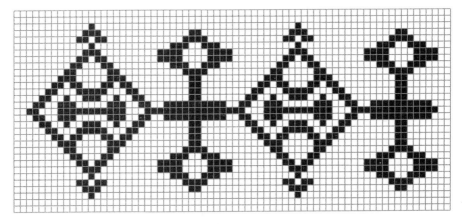

Fig. 64.
BORDER
Each design has 33 stitches.

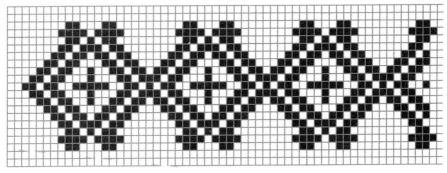

Fig. 65.
BORDER
Each design has 14 stitches.

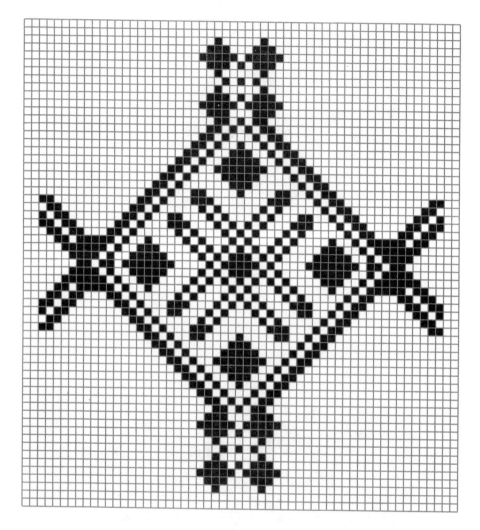

Fig. 66.

ORNAMENT

Each design has 52 stitches.

Fig. 67.
BORDER

Fig. 68.
SELBU STAR

Each design has 31 stitches.

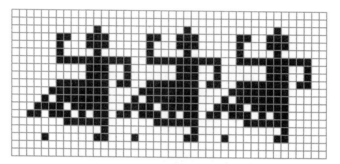

Fig. 69. KJERRING BORDER

(A Crone or a Dame)

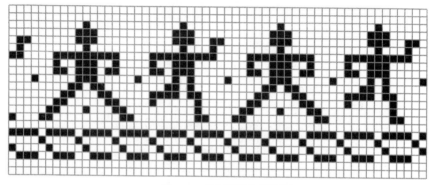

Fig. 70. DANSE BORDER

(Dance)

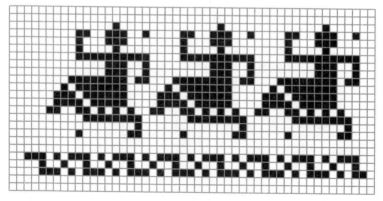

Fig. 71. KJERRING BORDER

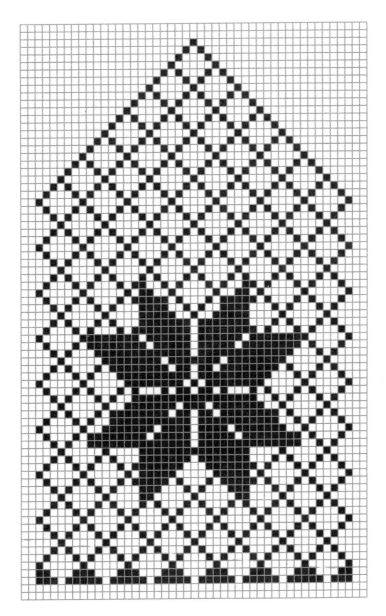

Fig. 72. HALLINGDAL MITTEN
Work a knit 2 purl 2 cuff. Suitable for the beginner.

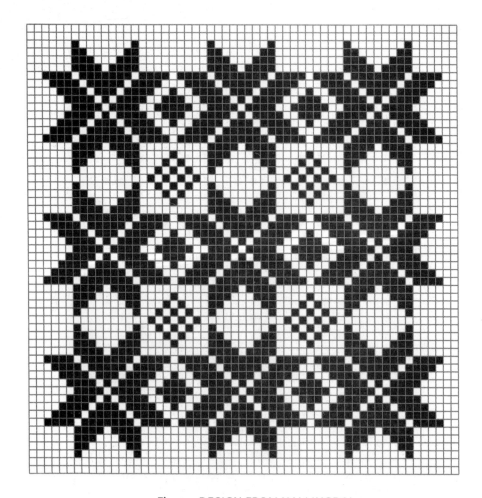

Fig. 73. DESIGN FROM HALLINGDAL

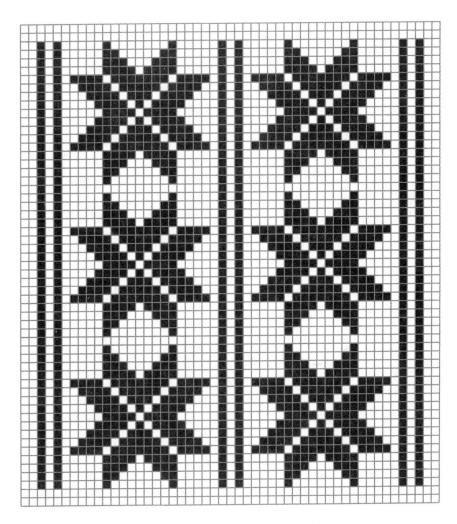

Fig. 74. DESIGN FROM HALLINGDAL

Fig. 75. OLD STYLE STOCKING

Fig. 76. MITTEN DESIGN FROM HALLINGDAL

Fig. 77. MITTEN DESIGN FROM HALLINGDAL

C A P

2 oz. Black wool, little bit of white and red wool of the same thickness, 5 sock needles number 12.

Cast on 110 stitches black wool, knit band (1 knit, 1 purl) for 1 inch, Knit 3 rounds black. In knitting the design use red and black the first three rounds. Remove the red and begin the star border, using white as the background with black stars. We complete the design as we began with the first red and black design. Now we continue knitting using black wool until the cap measures 9

inches. Cast off every other stitch during the next two rounds, cast off. Draw the stitches togther and sew firmly.

Make a large tassel using red, black and white wool. Press cap. for a child's cap cat on 100 stitches.

Ounces - oz

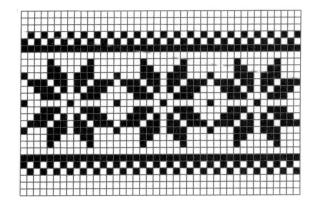

L U S K O F T E N

This knitted sweater is a modernized version of the ancient Norwegian "Luskofte" shown on page 39, the bottom of which is tucked into the trousers. Of course we would like the sweater to be loose and comfortable, therefore in using the old design, I have endeavored to compose a sweater to suit our own times. I have knitted it in the original colors—charcoal and white. The embroidery is worked in clear, bright shades of red, green and white on black background, thus the effect is better than if the sweater itself was of many colors. The finished embroidery or the material with traced design and embroidery yarn can be obtained on order from the Norwegian Home Craft Company, Oslo.

No. 1

> Wool - charcoal 13 oz
> white 3 oz.
> 1 round needle number 12,
> 5 sock needles number 12.

Using the charcoal wool cast on 260 stitches and knit waistband (1 knit 1 purl) 2 1/4 inches. Three rounds knit, then we begin using the white wool. Place both colors over the index finger of left hand, knit 3 charcoal s., 1 white s., 3 charcoal s., 1 white s. for one round. Be sure the wool follows loosely on the reverse side of the work. If one is not careful about this the right side of the garment will be marred by small bulges caused by the tautness of the white wool stretched over the charcoal stitches. Now three rounds of charcoal. Fourth round every fourth stitch is white. Be careful to have the white stitches of this

round directly above the middle charcoal stitch on the previous charcoal and white round. See diagram.

Knit this pattern for 15 inches. Before beginning on the armholes we can decide which method to use: we can knit the shoulder pieces in two ways, either by dividing the work in two with 130 stitches for the front and 130 for the back and knit the design Fig 1 back and forth every other row, alternating 1 row knit, 1 row purl, or we can continue knitting the design Fig. 1 on the round needles right up to the shoulder. This is much faster, but we must sew by machine, using very small stitches, twice around the arm opening.

No. 2

Then we very carefuly cut a slash be- tweeen the machine seams, straight down from the shoulder for 10 1/2 inches.

When one has come to the shoulder, by using one or other of these methods, cast off, press the work flat and divide stitches 7 inches on each shoulder and 6 1/2 inches for the neck. Sew the shoulder seams together.

Sleeves: Cast on 112 stitches on 4 sock needles, knit five rounds charcoal. This narrow band is used to cover the armhole seam when the garment is mounted. Continue knitting the design shown on Fig 2. Every 5th round decrease 1 stitch on both sides of the needle under the arm. Now we must be careful to maintain the design in spite of removing the stitches. We decrease every 5th row for the first 8 inches, then we decrease every 9th round. When the sleeve

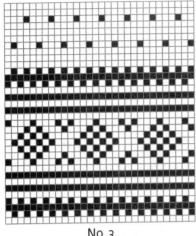

No. 3

measures 15 inches knit design on Fig. 3. If we are going to have embroidery on the wrist we knit another 4 inches then cast off loosely.

If embroidery is not going to be used we knit a wrist band for 4 inches (1 k. 1 p.), as well as a band around the neck. Remember to always cast off loosely, otherwise it will be diffficult to pull the sweater over the head.

The pressing is especially important. The design is much more attractive and distinct on a well-pressed garment.

ESKIMO

Wool

13 oz. black wool

3 oz. white

round needle nr. 12

5 sock needles nr. 12.

This sweater is simple and knits up very quickly because it is mostly plain knitting. The woman's sweater pictured is a small size.

Start with 4 sock needles and cast on 105 stitches loosely, so it will be easy to remove over the head. Knit 20 rounds for neck band (1 knit, 1 purl). Now we have reached "A" on Fig 1 and we begin the design. There are 15 such patterns around the neck, and be sure to increase 1 stitch on each

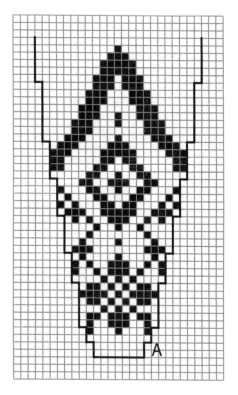

No. 1

of the design every time the drawing goes out of a square. When the points of the design are completed remove the white wool and knit 30 rounds plain knitting. We now have 375 stitches altogether - 105 stitches for the back, 75 for the right sleeve, 120 stitches for the front, and 75 stitches for the left sleeve. See Fig. 3.

Knit the 105 stitches back and forth and increase 1 stitch at the end of each row until there are 125 stitches on the needle. The 120 stitches for the front are increased in the same way until 140 stitches.

Remove the 75 stitches for each sleve on to two pieces of thread. Continue

knitting the 125 stitches + 140 stitches for 11 1/2 inches, then a waist band border of knit 1, purl 1 for 2 inches. Cast off loosely.

Sleeves: Pick up stitches for sleeves and knit back and forth, increasing 1 stitch at the end of each row under the arm until there are 86 stitches on the needle. Divide stitches on to sock needles and knit 11 inches. Now we begin the small design on the lower part of the sleeve, followed by 4 rounds of black.

We decrease now every other stitch until there are 48 stitches left. The sleeve is finished off with a 3 inch wrist band (1 knit, 1 purl).

We how now have an opening in the sleeve and therefore we knit a small 2 1/4 inch square which we press and insert.

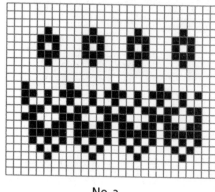

No. 2

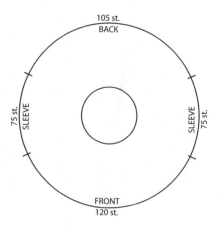

No. 3

Using the Charts

Charted designs can be used in a wide range of techniques: knitting, of course, but also filet crochet, bead weaving, needlepoint and counted cross stitch. Designs can also be traced and rounded, for use in other media like crewel embroidery, paper arts, or even painted in a folk art style.

Stranded Knitting

Whole volumes have been written on two-color knitting, and I recommend the reader refer to the reading list at the end of this section. Norwegian designs, being worked in two colors of strong contrast, should be worked with the color not in use stranded loosely across the back, and should never be woven into the wrong side of the knitting. Weaving in will always permit a tiny bit of the other color to show through on the right side. In fair isle knitting, where the colors are always changing, this may not be noticeable, but even the slightest haze of black showing through a white block will make the piece look dirty. Just don't do it.

Designing Your Piece

The easiest way to use these charts is to substitute them into an existing pattern. For example, if you have a knit hat pattern with a stranded design that has a repeat of 10 sts, you can find (or create) your own 10 st chart and use that instead.

To create your own design from scratch, taking inspiration from the charts, is only a little more complicated. Again, you can refer to an existing pattern for dimensions of the final product, count your chart, and adjust the number of stitches you cast on accordingly. For example, if you have a pullover pattern that fits well, and has a stitch count of 320 stitches, you can find or design a chart that, when repeated, adds up to a number close to 320, cast on that number, and work in your design, following the schematic of the existing pattern as you go. It's not cheating, and the difference in fit between 320 sts and 312 will be negligible when you block the piece on completion.

Symbolism

Folk art is most pleasing, and most powerful, when the designs used have symbolic meaning, and the finished work conveys a message to both the creator and the viewer. Symbols point to a reality larger than what they seem to represent. You can research the old meanings for symbols, and this is a good place to start, but more important is what the designs mean to you.

I have three cats, at the time of publication. Recently, one of my cats became very ill. The veterinarian found that her heart was failing. While she was in the hospital I designed and knit a mitten using hearts, flowering sprigs, cats, and a zigzag pattern I created specifically to look like a cardiac chart. The hearts represented her ailment as well as my love for her. The flowering branches were for growth, that her heart would recover. The cats and cardiac chart again, represented her specifically and her specific medical condition.

As I knit the mitten, I thought about her sweet personality; my mitten became a meditation, and a prayer, for her recovery. For the record, she has recovered from the immediate heart failure. She will be on medication for the rest of her life, but as far as we can tell, that life won't be shortened in any significant way. I don't know that my knitting healed my cat, but it healed me, and helped me through a very rough few days of worrying. And that was good enough.

As you create your new designs, think about what is happening in your life right now, and what you would like to have happen. Using designs to try to manipulate the universe into meeting your immediate demands will probably fail, but using them to discover and align your interests with the universe can be extremely powerful. This is the difference between magic and meditation.

Folk motifs have roots in and operate in the realm that Jung called the collective unconscious, and this is always changing, so our interpretation of symbols is always changing, too. The pirate's Jolly Roger caused terror on the 17th century high seas, but today more often represents individuality unchained from conventional thinking. The ancient sun-wheel was a powerful life symbol until it was corrupted into the Nazi swastika. We are always creating new designs and new associations that are as powerful as the ancient ones, and symbols that mean one thing to one person can mean something entirely different to another. Or to yourself at different stages of life. Does a robot represent the mechanized world taking over, or is it a helpful companion? We are always meditating on something; most often mundane concerns like money, or relationships, or household chores. When we center ourselves by intentionally meditating on symbols that hold great meaning for US, in alignment with what we can discover of universal principals of harmony and life, we put that symbol's energy back into the collective unconsiousness.

Color

Color is just as powerful as the pictoral elements of your design. Publishing in black and white requires strong contrast, so I have knit the samples in simple dark and light values. You should use colors that reinforce the meanings of your symbols, or add in some way. For example, my kitty mitten is worked in a background of grey, because my cat is grey. I wanted to use green to match her eyes, for the pattern color, but I didn't have the right shade, so I used light blue instead. If you were desiging a piece in a checkboard pattern, and were reminded of a red checkerboard blanket your mother always brought to picnics, you could work your piece in red, and it would tap into the feelings you had at your family picnics. So a hat or bag or whatever you were making, could become a meditation on family, on happy times, good food, playing with your family and friends. When you use that piece, you will be bringing those associations along with you.

Designing art must not be limited to professional artists. In our earliest history, everyone was an artist. And you are, too. You express your self in everything that you make. Using symbols and colors that remind the knitter of life, and of love, and peace, we can make the world just a little bit better. One mitten at a time.

Original knitting pattern, Kitty Selbu, is available from my Ravelry shop at http://www.ravelry.com/designers/terri-shea

Other Books You Might Enjoy

Invisible Threads in Knitting by Annemor Sundbø
Everyday Knitting by Annemor Sundbø
Setesdal Sweaters by Annemor Sundbø
Selbuvotter: Biography of a Knitting Tradition by Terri Shea
Alice Starmore's Book of Fair Isle Knitting by Alice Starmore
Poems of Color: Knitting in the Bohus Tradition by Wendy Keele
The Art of Fair Isle Knitting by Ann Feitelson
Fabulous Fair Isle by John Allen
Fancy Feet by Anna Zilbourg
Folk Knitting in Estonia by Nancy Bush
Traditional Scandinavian Knitting by Sheila McGregor
Traditional Fair Isle Knitting by Sheila McGregor
A History of Hand Knitting by Richard Rutt